a guide to

LONDON

by

WEEKEND JOURNALS

WORDS
Milly Kenny-Ryder

DESIGN
Simon Lovell

PHOTOGRAPHY
Gabriel Kenny-Ryder

weekendjournals.co.uk

CONTENTS

—

Our chosen places take you on a journey across London, from Richmond in the southwest to Hackney in the northeast.

PREFACE

—

London has always been home for me. I grew up in the leafy suburbs of West London and now reside south of the river in the ever-evolving borough of Southwark. Each is an urban village while being part of the wonderfully diverse conurbation that is Greater London. The sprawling city is impossible to comprehend in one day, in fact you could spend decades getting to know the historic streets and iconic landmarks, and still have exciting places left to discover.

There is something new to try in the capital every week with a cultural and culinary scene that is as vibrant as any other city in the world, but the older parts of this metropolis are perhaps the most magical and memorable. Over the last ten years of writing about London, I have ventured to all corners of the city to keep my online diary up to date with the latest and best discoveries.

Everyone who lives in London will have a list of favourite eateries, shops, parks and museums in their neighbourhood, but may not often travel further afield. In this journal I hope to give you an insight into my 'little black book', with recommendations to keep both Londoners and visitors busy and entertained. From celebrated institutions to trendsetting newcomers, there is an eclectic variety to satisfy every budget, appetite and itinerary.

Milly Kenny-Ryder

LONDON LANDMARKS

—

Numbers on map overleaf

MUSEUMS & GALLERIES

1   Natural History Museum
2   Royal Academy of Arts
3   Tate Modern
4   The British Museum
5   The National Gallery
6   The V&A

SIGHTS

7   Big Ben
8   Buckingham Palace
9   Marble Arch
10   St Paul's Cathedral
11   The London Eye
12   Tower Bridge
13   Tower of London
14   Trafalgar Square

SHOPS

15   Fortnum & Mason
16   Harrods
17   Liberty London
18   Selfridges

THEATRES

19   National Theatre
20   Royal Albert Hall
21   Royal Opera House

MARKETS

22   Borough
23   Columbia Road
24   Portobello
25   Spitalfields

MAP OF LONDON

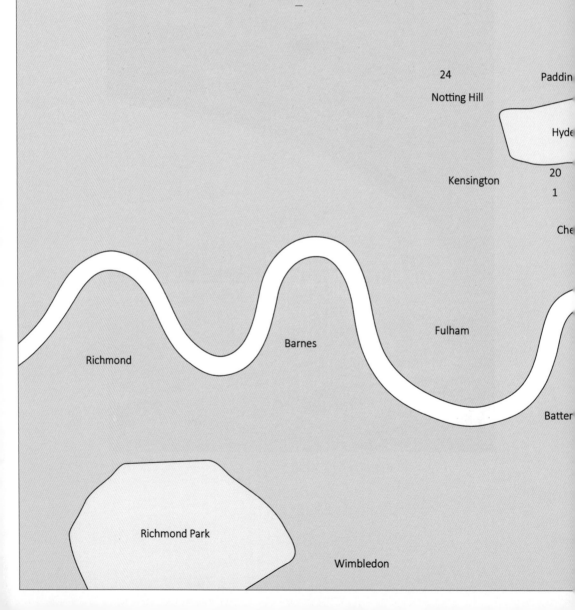

24
Notting Hill

Paddin

Hyde

Kensington

20

1

Che

Barnes

Fulham

Richmond

Batter

Richmond Park

Wimbledon

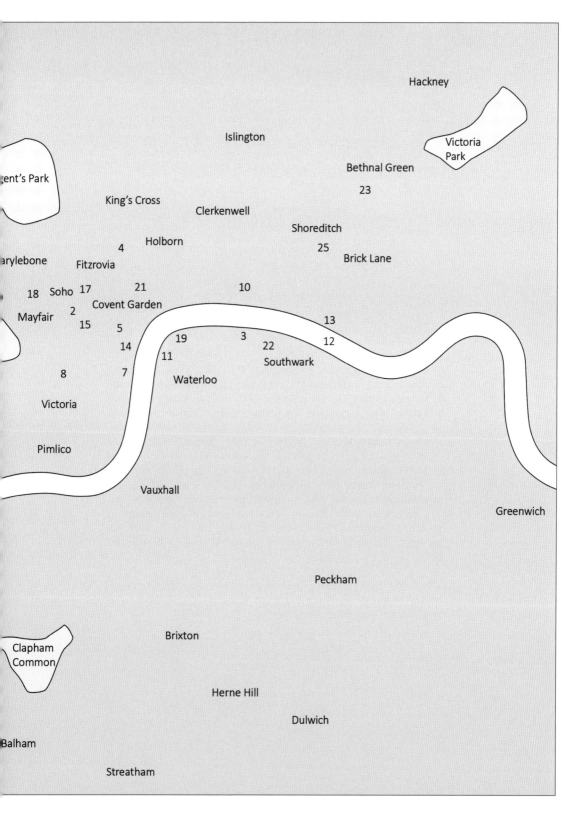

ROYAL BOTANIC GARDENS, KEW

—

Gardens

Kew, Richmond, TW9 3AE
020 8332 5655
kew.org

When the weather is good in London, Kew Gardens is one of the most glorious places to spend your time. Located in the West London borough of Richmond, there are over 130 hectares of rich landscape to explore and plenty to keep younger visitors entertained.

The Royal Botanic Gardens, founded in 1759, contain the largest and most diverse collection of plants in the world and are truly deserving of their UNESCO World Heritage Site status. Wander through the monumental tropical greenhouses or engage with the geometric Hive, a sensory installation that aims to highlight the extraordinary life of bees. Culture fans will enjoy learning about the history of Kew Palace, the former residence of King George III, while more daring visitors will find the treetop walkway thrilling with its panoramic views of the greenery below.

Whether you are fanatical about flowers, a keen explorer or just enjoy natural beauty, there is something for everyone at Kew Gardens, an idyllic escape from the chaos of the city.

OLYMPIC STUDIOS

—

Cinema

117-123 Church Road, Barnes, SW13 9HL
020 8912 5161
olympicstudios.co.uk

Barnes is a quiet and leafy neighbourhood of West London. There are plenty of green spaces, cute cafés, and you will also find Olympic Studios, a retro cinema, restaurant and members' club.

The building first opened in 1906 as an entertainment hall and was later used as a cinema and recording studio. The studios were a mecca for some of the world's most famous rock stars including Led Zeppelin, Queen and Pink Floyd. The legendary venue re-opened as a luxury cinema in 2013, with a charming ground floor bistro and a stylish members' bar and lounge upstairs.

Olympic Studios has two screens, both kitted out with super comfortable woolfelt reclining seats from Norway and the highest quality Dolby sound systems. There are custom made tables perfect for holding a classic cocktail or box of popcorn.

Across the road, the Olympic Studios team have opened a record shop, where music lovers can peruse the collection of vintage vinyls.

STORY

—

Coffee Shop

115 St John's Hill, Battersea, SW11 1SZ
020 7998 3303
storycoffee.co.uk

With so many speciality coffee shops across London it is difficult to know where to quench your caffeine cravings. Story is the place to go in Battersea, conveniently close to the chaotic Clapham Junction station, but far enough away to feel calm and laid-back.

The petite café has found a home in a charming corner spot and has a nostalgic, retro custard sign printed on the wall above the entrance. St John's Hill is a little community, and appealing shops and restaurants surround Story.

The interiors are carefully designed to make the most of the small space. One tree trunk has been used for all the furniture and decor, and the honeycomb bar is particularly striking. The husband and wife team proudly serve Square Mile Coffee, while a short menu of brunch favourites is available all day.

MILK

—

Café & Restaurant

18-20 Bedford Hill, Balham, SW12 9RG
020 8772 9085
milk.london

Balham has been a better place to eat since Milk opened in the neighbourhood. This destination café was created by Julian Porter and Lauren Johns and has an Australian vibe. Their smiling team proudly serve carefully chosen speciality coffee and irresistible brunch dishes.

The light and airy café is relaxed but chic, with rustic wooden tables and retro branding. The café is always busy, often with a queue out the door, but the moreish food and expertly made coffee is worth the wait.

Everything on the menu is delicious, from baked eggs to soft-serve ice cream. Don't miss the special weekend buckwheat pancakes, which always arrive with a variety of beautiful toppings.

In the evenings, the café hosts collaborative dinners with guest chefs from some of the capital's best kitchens.

LLEWELYN'S

—

Restaurant

293–295 Railton Road, Herne Hill, SE24 0JP
020 7733 6676
llewelyns-restaurant.co.uk

Llewelyn's is reason alone to visit Herne Hill, a quaint neighbourhood in South London. The Victorian dining room is decorated in a minimalist style, but the staff bring a natural warmth to the atmosphere.

Next door to the train station, in a convivial local square, the restaurant has both indoor and outdoor seating, dependent on weather. General Manager Alcides Gauto will make you feel instantly at home, having gained experience in hospitality at industry hang-out Rochelle Canteen.

The menu is satisfyingly short, with a single sheet of paper offering a selection of tempting seasonal dishes. Head Chef, Warren Fleet, makes sophisticated comfort food championing great produce. Favourites like Griddled Sardines with chilli, garlic and parsley are often on the menu, but the kitchen also adds daily specials to the list. A selective drinks list has been carefully curated to showcase interesting and delicious wines, and there are always a few cocktails to choose from.

KRICKET

—

Restaurant

41-43 Atlantic Road, Brixton, SW9 8JL
020 3826 4090
kricket.co.uk/brixton

Indian cuisine is much-loved by Londoners and there is a huge variety of traditional and modern Indian restaurants to choose from. Whether you favour authentic, spicy Mughlai cuisine or light and aromatic Keralan dishes, you can find most regional varieties in every neighbourhood.

Kricket exploded onto London's food scene in 2015, when college friends Rik Campbell and Will Bowlby introduced their idea of inexpensive, small plates of Indian food to South London. Opening up in a cramped shipping container in Pop Brixton, the flavoursome grub was an instant hit, rivalling some of the finest Indian restaurants in the city.

Fans flocked to Brixton to queue for the addictively good Bhel Puri and Samphire Pakoras. As demand grew, the Kricket boys shut their temporary Brixton outpost and moved to a larger, more glamorous home in Soho. In 2018, Kricket re-opened a permanent eatery - with a bar and test kitchen - under the arches in Brixton and also a third restaurant in White City Television Centre. So whether you are in south, west or central London, you can get your Kricket kicks, but our favourite outpost is their atmospheric Brixton venue.

GENERAL STORE

—

Shop

174 Bellenden Road, Peckham, SE15 4BW
020 7642 2129
generalsto.re

Bellenden Road is at the heart of the creative activity in Peckham, with a row of innovative eateries, quirky shops and welcoming cafés.

General Store stands out, thanks to its charming façade with bunches of seasonal flowers or baskets of apples perched outside. The upmarket grocery store is owned by an enthusiastic and passionate duo, Merlin and Gena. They choose the finest honest and classic products, sourced from special producers and farmers in Britain and further afield, to fill the shelves of their small, but perfectly organised shop.

Wooden crates of abundant produce sit looking pretty in the centre of the room presenting the best of the season. The larder that lines the shop features some of the best, small British food brands; look out for Pump Street chocolate and preserves from Lillie O'Brien's London Borough of Jam.

General Store also offers great coffee and has a selection of tempting pastries and bread, so you can pop in for a drink or snack-to-go.

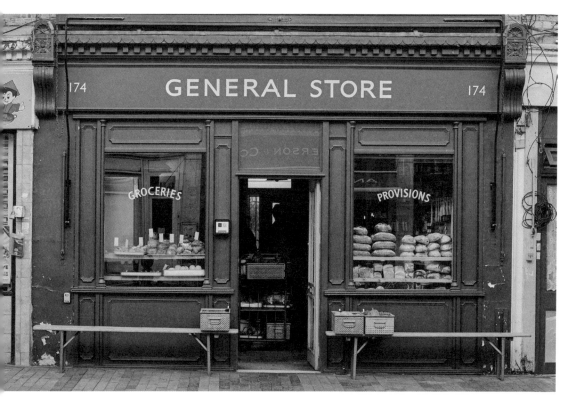

SOUTH LONDON GALLERY

—

Gallery

65-67 Peckham Road, Peckham, SE5 8UH
020 7703 6120
southlondongallery.org

Camberwell is one of the most exciting districts in London, with lots of events and creative venues opening every month.

The South London Gallery was established on its current site in 1891 by philanthropist William Rossiter to 'bring art to the people of South London'. It has expanded over the years and now, as well as the original venue, South London Gallery has several other spaces - including The Fire Station designed by 6a Architects - and gardens where they display a range of contemporary art for both adults and children.

Every year the gallery curators organise a range of free exhibitions showcasing exciting and intriguing contemporary art. While the solo shows focus on well-known British and international artists, group shows offer an opportunity to learn about lesser-known works. The galleries are bright and spacious, allowing the bold artwork to speak for itself.

The Habit Café at South London Gallery is a great place to refuel, with hearty brunch dishes, locally-roasted coffee, wine and craft beer.

ARTIST RESIDENCE

—

Hotel

52 Cambridge Street, Pimlico, SW1V 4QQ
020 3019 8610
artistresidence.co.uk

The Artist Residence family of hotels balances luxury accommodation with a fun, approachable style. Their hotels began in Brighton when artists were invited to decorate a room in exchange for accommodation. The owners Justin and Charlie continued to grow their group, adding boutique hotels in Cornwall, London and Oxfordshire to the collection. Each property has its own character while remaining true to the eclectic artistic style of the very first hotel.

In London, their charming hotel is found on Cambridge Street in Pimlico, conveniently close to Victoria Station and many of the city's most prominent sights.

There are ten unique bedrooms to choose from, kitted out with big beds and quirky artworks. Everybody's favourite room is the Grand Suite, a light and airy bedroom with photogenic furniture and a carefree, but luxurious vintage charm.

Breakfast, lunch and dinner are served in the hotel's resident restaurant, Cambridge Street Kitchen, and the atmospheric basement cocktail bar is fun for late night drinking.

THE DESIGN MUSEUM

—

Museum

224-238 Kensington High Street, Kensington, W8 6AG
020 3862 5900
designmuseum.org

The Design Museum is bigger and better than ever before since its move to West London in 2016. It is housed in the former Commonwealth Institute on Kensington High Street, a landmark building dating back to the 1960s. John Pawson designed the museum's minimalist interior, a spacious ground floor atrium with exposed stairs leading up to the other floors.

The museum is devoted to design of all kinds, covering products, architecture, fashion and graphics. Each exhibition celebrates an aspect of visual invention and is constructed to appeal to visitors of all ages. On the top floor the permanent collection, Designer Maker User, is displayed with key objects and artefacts. There is also a restaurant and reference library.

Other floors host regular temporary exhibitions and events. The annual Beazley Designs of the Year exhibition is a highlight of the museum's programme, when the world's most innovative and exciting new designs from the past year are on display.

NATIVE & CO

Shop

116 Kensington Park Road, Notting Hill, W11 2PW
020 7243 0418
nativeandco.com

You will always find Native & Co perfectly ordered and immaculately tidy. This tiny, speciality design store in Notting Hill is co-owned by Sharon Jo-Yun Hung and Chris Yoshiro Green, who both studied product design at Central Saint Martins before opening their charming boutique. The duo sources items from artisanal makers and traditional craftsmen in Japan and Taiwan, as well as designing and selling their own range of homeware.

The shelves are home to a range of beautifully simple and practical objects of desire, from ceramics to utensils, textiles to trinkets. The items all have one thing in common, being true to their native origin. Visit this collection to admire the stylish wares and maybe walk away with an unusual treasure that will complement any home.

CORE

—

Restaurant

92 Kensington Park Road, Notting Hill, W11 2PN
020 3937 5086
corebyclaresmyth.com

Clare Smyth has learnt her craft in the kitchens of some of the best restaurants in the world, most notably Gordon Ramsay's flagship in Chelsea, where she became the first and only female chef to hold three Michelin stars. Her first solo venture, Core, offers a sensational, fresh and understated dining experience, with an emphasis on natural, modest ingredients.

Nestled among the substantial villas of Kensington Park Road in Notting Hill, this sophisticated eatery feels very much at home. The dining room is elegant but relaxed, with simple foliage adorning the tables and a clean, minimal decor.

Guests can choose three courses from the à la carte, or opt for the embellished tasting menus. Although the dishes shift according to the season, signatures include the Lemonade Parfait dessert, a striking sweet dish with fizzy citrus notes and the warmth of honey.

THE PILGRM

—

Hotel

25 London Street, Paddington, W2 1HH
020 7667 6000
thepilgrm.com

Paddington might not be the first place you would choose to stay in London, even though the area is busy with tourists who have come into the major train station. The Pilgrm Hotel, a cool and discreet establishment in the heart of the district, has changed that.

The building was stripped back to reveal original details before being transformed into the stylish boutique hotel you see today. The 73 rooms, though compact, are perfectly designed with bespoke features and hand-picked materials. Simplicity reigns in the bedrooms, with crisp white bed sheets, striking black lampshades and leafy plant additions.

Reacting against hotel conventions, there is no reception desk or standard check-in, instead you are encouraged to be immediately immersed in the homely environment. Downstairs, a Workshop Coffee café is a brilliant place to linger in the mornings, while the glamorous lounge upstairs features a menu by ex-Grain Store chef Sara Lewis.

With rooms for less than £100, this is a rare opportunity to stay somewhere in London that is affordable and convenient while being wonderfully chic.

SERPENTINE GALLERIES

—

Gallery

Kensington Gardens, W2 3XA
020 7402 6075
serpentinegalleries.org

Hyde Park is undoubtedly London's most popular park. There are over 350 acres of verdant greenery, a lake with pedal-boats, regular music events and the Serpentine Gallery, situated in the neighbouring Kensington Gardens.

The Serpentine actually has two spaces within Kensington Gardens (The Serpentine Gallery and The Serpentine Sackler Gallery); both exhibit important, contemporary art. Admission to both is free for all.

The Serpentine Gallery is a former tea pavilion, built in 1933 and designed by architect James Grey West. In recent years, notable artists on display have included Paula Rego, Anish Kapoor and John Latham. The Serpentine Sackler Gallery opened in 2013 and was designed by world-renowned architect Dame Zaha Hadid.

Each summer a much-anticipated temporary Pavilion, designed by a prestigious artist or architect, is constructed in the gardens.

POSTCARD TEAS

—

Shop

9 Dering Street, Mayfair, W1S 1AG
020 7629 3654
postcardteas.com

Although the British are known for their love of tea, it is difficult to find places in the capital to buy high quality, unique blends. Postcard Teas is centrally located, just off Bond Street, and is a tiny boutique specialising in loose leaf teas from all over the world.

Husband and wife team Timothy and Asako d'Offay have a great passion for fine teas and have travelled extensively, discovering small producers all over the world. Some of the family producers in China, Japan, Taiwan, Korea and Vietnam have only an acre or two, but the d'Offays are eager to showcase the unique flavour profiles while also supporting these independent growers.

In the store, you can try a selection from the Postcard Teas collection, including a variety of classic London blends. Buy a beautiful caddy of exemplary Earl Grey for yourself, or send a box to a friend via the shop's postcard delivery service.

Tea lovers can also invest in carefully curated tea paraphernalia; most luxurious perhaps are the Kaikado tin tea caddies, which are handmade in Kyoto.

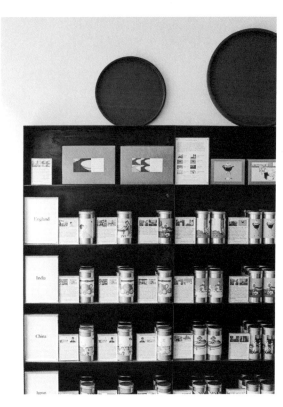

HÉLÈNE DARROZE AT
THE CONNAUGHT

—

Restaurant

The Connaught, Carlos Place, Mayfair, W1K 2AL
020 3147 7200
the-connaught.co.uk

It is easy to get confused by London's fine dining scene. There are restaurants for every occasion and every budget, but only a handful are really worth the high-end hype. Hélène Darroze at The Connaught stands out, with reliably excellent food and service to match.

The Connaught in Mayfair is renowned as one of London's top hotels, with an award-winning bar and extravagant bedrooms. It is unsurprising, therefore, to find one of London's finest restaurants residing within.

Darroze hails from the Basque region of France, a produce-rich area with a strong culinary heritage. Her two Michelin-starred restaurant offers classic Basque dishes reinvented in a modern and inventive way. The results are aesthetically appealing, flavourful plates of food.

THOMAS'S CAFÉ AT BURBERRY

—

Café

5 Vigo Street, Mayfair, W1S 3HA
020 3159 1410
uk.burberry.com/stores/thomass-cafe

Those in the know hold their breakfast and lunch meetings at the all-day dining destination, Thomas's Café at Burberry. Tucked away in the Burberry flagship store on Regent Street, this stylish café is a luxurious place to spend a mealtime or coffee break.

The unassuming venue opened in 2015, named after the fashion brand's Founder, Thomas Burberry. It is an escape from the hustle and bustle of Mayfair, minutes away from Oxford Street and Piccadilly Circus. Inside, the design is in keeping with Burberry's classic British elegance. Downstairs, surrounded by luxury accessories and desirable handbags, the friendly, Scandi-inspired café is ideal for a quiet cup of tea. For longer meals there is a lovely light dining room upstairs, kitted out with sage green velvet seating, a beautiful tiled floor and mid-century details.

Menus at Thomas's Café at Burberry are thankfully short and wonderfully nostalgic. Highlights include homemade crumpets - served hot from the AGA - for breakfast, and lobster and chips with a glass of champagne for lunch.

PERFUMER H

—

Shop

106a Crawford Street, Marylebone, W1H 2HZ
020 7258 7859
perfumerh.com

Perfumer H quietly occupies a corner of Crawford Street in Marylebone. This chic, understated shop is a sensual haven for scent lovers. There is a warmth and cosiness, thanks to the teak and polished brass decor, and hand-blown glass vessels by Michael Ruh glow on the shelves. Visitors will feel encouraged to explore Perfumer H's aromas, their seasonal editions and the library collection of perfumes past.

The brains - and nose - behind the operation is Lyn Harris, the talent who founded international perfume brand, Miller Harris. After making a name for herself in the world of beauty, she opened Perfumer H in 2015 as a laboratory and store enabling her to freely experiment and create. The majority of Lyn's perfumes are inspired by natural aromas: think Dandelion, Suede, Marmalade; many are memories from her childhood growing up in Yorkshire and a love of the transient, changing seasons.

Let Lyn and her experienced team help you find your fragrance or, for something even more special, Lyn will work with you to design a bespoke scent that matches every facet of your life and personality.

ROGANIC

—

Restaurant

5-7 Blandford Street, Marylebone, W1U 3DB
020 3370 6260
roganic.uk

Simon Rogan's flagship restaurant L'Enclume, in the Lake District, is often named as one of the best in the country, renowned for its sensitive and innovative handling of ingredients from its own farm.

Roganic first opened in London in 2011, for a two year residency in Marylebone. The concept returned in 2018, setting up a civilised dining room on Blandford Street. The eatery is laid out with simple wooden tables, decorative Tom Raffield lightshades and a pop of colour from the deep orange leather banquettes.

Head Chef Oli Marlow and his team create an imaginative 11-course tasting menu, showcasing produce from their farm in the Lake District. For a more succinct offering, opt for the affordable four-course lunch, which is equally delicious. The menus change regularly but have included delicate flavour combinations such as 'almond, scallop, apple' and 'peach, figleaf, apple marigold'. The friendly staff are more than willing to suggest unusual but brilliant drinks pairings.

For an insider experience book a space at Aulis in Soho, Rogan's experimental chef's table for just eight diners.

ANOTHER COUNTRY

—

Shop

18 Crawford Street, Marylebone, W1H 1BT
020 7486 3251
anothercountry.com

Another Country is one of the many aesthetically appealing shops in Marylebone. The beautifully ordered shop stocks inspirational design brands from around the world, alongside its own functional and stylish craft furniture.

Owner Paul de Zwart previously co-founded Wallpaper Magazine before opening Another Country as a place to promote his sustainable and timeless furniture and accessories. The pieces are influenced by Japanese wood-making and Scandinavian mid-century design.

The small showroom in Marylebone is split over two floors, with elegant sofas and chairs taking centre stage. Other important brands include Workstead lighting, Crane kitchenware and David Mellor classic cutlery.

The shop has a harmonious feel, with every piece deserving recognition for its considered design and beautiful simplicity. In short, Another Country has everything you could need to create a lovely home.

THE WALLACE COLLECTION

—

Museum

Hertford House, Manchester Square, Marylebone, W1U 3BN
020 7563 9500
wallacecollection.org

Hertford House, tucked away on Manchester Square just behind Oxford Street, is home to the majestic Wallace Collection; a free to wander and explore museum with over 6,000 works of art, largely dating from the 15th to the 19th century.

The museum's collection was donated to the British public by Sir Richard Wallace, the illegitimate son of an aristocratic family who owned large properties across the country. It is based in Hertford House, a wonderfully lavish mansion, with a grand façade and opulent interior.

The entrance hall reveals a spectacular staircase that leads visitors up to a sweep of regal, highly decorated rooms, each with its own character and style. The walls proudly display some of Europe's best known masters: dramatic paintings by Rembrandt, Titian and Gainsborough. The Wallace Collection is perhaps best known for its unrivalled collection of French painting and decorative art, including favourites by Watteau, Boucher and Fragonard.

The Wallace Collection has an airy courtyard brasserie and a basement exhibition space, which hosts temporary shows throughout the year.

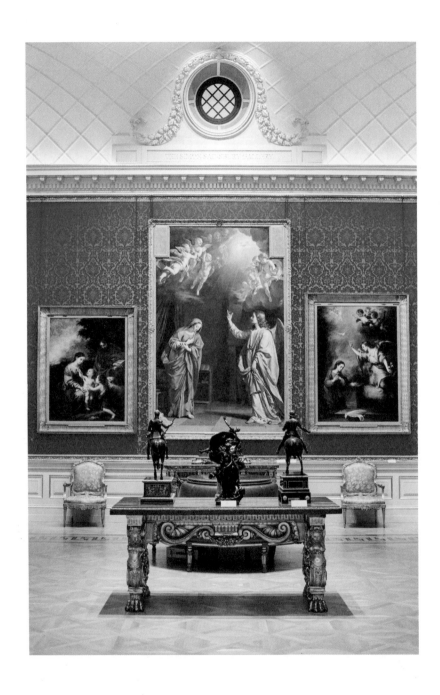

MARGARET HOWELL

—

Shop

34 Wigmore Street, Marylebone, WIU 2RS
020 7009 9009
margarethowell.co.uk

Margaret Howell is a hero of the British fashion world. For over four decades she has presented menswear and womenswear that is immaculately tailored and effortlessly classic.

After studying at Goldsmiths, Margaret Howell began creating her own accessories and shirts, before opening her first franchise shop on South Molton Street in 1976. Her independent stand-alone boutique followed four years later on St Christopher's Place. Margaret Howell's flagship is now found on Wigmore Street and there are several other boutiques around London.

Margaret Howell's collections are remarkably timeless, with comfort and practicality at the heart. Expect to find beautifully fitting, flattering trousers and artfully tailored shirts. The collections are inspired by nature and landscape, and Margaret Howell is adamant about working with skilled, thoughtful manufacturers. The brand's diffusion line, MHL, showcases garments that are similar in style but more affordable in price.

LINA STORES

—

Restaurant

51 Greek Street, Soho, W1D 4EH
020 3929 0068
linastores.co.uk

The original Lina Stores, on Brewer Street, has been a popular resident of Soho since opening in 1944. Fans of Italian food flock to the tiny turquoise corner shop to stock up on homemade pasta, olive oil and panettone.

In 2018, this institution opened a fresh pasta restaurant on nearby Greek Street. The restaurant follows the same recognisable branding, with a retro turquoise bar and open kitchen. Pasta is delivered daily from their Brewer Street store or made in-house by chef Masha Rener.

The menu is simple and seductive with reasonably priced plates of pasta and flavoursome starters. The Gnudi con Burro e Salvia is addictively tasty, especially when accompanied with a strong Lina Stores Negroni. Save room for dessert as Lina Stores pride themselves on serving the best chocolate tart in London. The Torta al Cioccolato is somehow blissfully light but indulgently rich, and not to be missed.

KETTNER'S TOWNHOUSE
—
Hotel

29 Romilly Street, Soho, W1D 5HP
020 7734 5650
kettnerstownhouse.com

There was a lot of buzz in Soho when Kettner's Townhouse opened in early 2018. Kettner's, originally opened in 1867, was an iconic French restaurant for over 150 years before its closure in 2015.

On-trend hospitality giant Soho House acquired the property and transformed the site into a charming luxury hotel, ideally located for those wishing to stay somewhere special in central London.

Alongside the sociable bistro and champagne bar, there are 33 beautifully designed bedrooms to choose from. Where possible, original features have been restored with Georgian floorboards, Art Deco chandeliers and antique fireplaces. Although each room is different, all have an alluring 1920s feel. The medium-sized rooms on the top floor are particularly lovely, with plenty of natural light and luxurious roll-top bathtubs.

Unlike some of the members-only Soho House properties, Kettner's Townhouse is open to all, but members do receive a discount on rooms.

BAO

—

Restaurant

53 Lexington Street, Soho, W1F 9AS
baolondon.com

It is hard to remember a time when bao buns didn't exist on menus in London. The magical, milk steamed buns hit the food scene hard and Taiwanese eateries are continuing to open across the capital. The trend is all thanks to Bao, which started as a tiny pop-up food stall in East London's Netil Market, offering a short menu of comforting, filled fluffy buns.

Bao was founded by Shing Tat Chung, his wife Erchen Chang and sister Wai Ting Chung. Their permanent Soho eatery opened in 2015, followed by a second site in Fitzrovia a few years later. The team now also have Xu, a teahouse and restaurant inspired by the luxury 1930s dining rooms of Taipei. All three restaurants are worth a visit, but the Soho branch feels the most authentic and the constant queue outside indicates its ongoing popularity.

Found on Lexington Street, Bao Soho is a tiny venue with a simple but beautifully designed dining room. The short menu lists a variety of filled buns and small Taiwanese plates and rice bowls. Don't miss the Classic Bao and the Trotter Nuggets.

THE LONDON EDITION

—

Hotel

10 Berners Street, Fitzrovia, W1T 3NP
020 7781 0000
editionhotels.com/london

Moments away from Oxford Circus, The London Edition Hotel is located in the very heart of the capital.

The 19th century building is immediately impressive as you enter. A high-ceilinged, stucco entrance hall features dramatic artwork and a lavish bar for guests or visitors to unwind with a drink. Adjacent is a magnificent dining room, called Berners Tavern, that showcases the food of Jason Atherton. The secret Punch Room is a cosy and alluring bar, serving a range of inventive punch recipes.

Upstairs, the bedrooms are minimalist and modern, with walnut-panelled walls and oak floors giving a luxurious warmth to the space. In the suites, decadent details include George Smith sofas and gold-framed photographs from Hendrik Kerstens.

There is everything you need within the hotel, but should you wish to venture outside, Fitzrovia is awash with in-vogue eateries and shops.

CHOOSING KEEPING

—

Shop

21 Tower Street, Covent Garden, WC2H 9NS
020 7613 3842
choosingkeeping.com

Choosing Keeping offers a charming collection of stationery gems from makers around the world. The shop, found in Seven Dials in Covent Garden, is a colourful emporium of desk paraphernalia including limited edition scissors from Italy, artistic French notebooks and beautiful handmade celluloid Cherry Tree fountain pens from Japan. All of this is displayed alongside Choosing Keeping's beautiful own-brand products.

The owner, Julia, organises the carefully sourced items in a meticulous but eclectic style; you could happily explore and examine the shop for hours. Stationery addicts will delight at the shelves of perfectly stacked marbled boxes, colour coordinated pots of pencils, and pretty cards for every occasion. This intriguing gallery of curiosities will appeal to everyone, whether a collector, a correspondent or just a penpal.

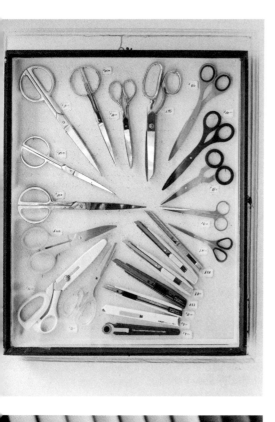

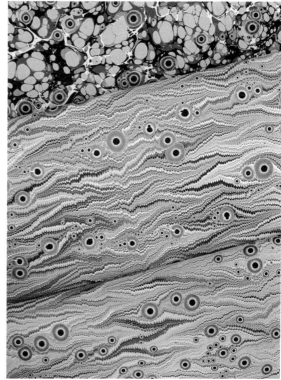

HENRIETTA HOTEL

—

Hotel

14-15 Henrietta Street, Covent Garden, WC2E 8QH
020 3794 5313
henriettahotel.com

Nestling among the stylish boutiques and restaurants of Covent Garden is Henrietta Hotel. The 18-room hotel is the first from French company Experimental Group, who own a collection of restaurants and bars across Europe and New York.

Henrietta Hotel has a quaint, neighbourhood feel, perhaps thanks to its home within two adjoining Victorian townhouses. Downstairs, an upscale restaurant is run by chef Sylvain Roucayrol, whose menu of playful dishes is inspired by Southwest France and the Basque region. Pick from the flavoursome small plates and accompany with a creative cocktail from the bar.

The bedrooms are found upstairs, spread across five floors, and are of varying sizes and shapes. All rooms have a relaxed vintage vibe mixed with millennial pink and deep maroon hues. Heavy curtains keep the rooms dark and quiet at night and reveal historic views of Covent Garden when opened. The striking headboards, from designer Dorothée Meilichzon, have become the signature of this boutique hotel.

COLEMAN COFFEE ROASTERS
—
Coffee Shop

20 Lower Marsh, Waterloo, SE1 7RJ
020 3267 1139
colemancoffee.com

Waterloo commuters rejoiced when Coleman Coffee Roasters opened on Lower Marsh in early 2016. This speciality coffee shop was the first of its kind in the area and is always full of caffeine-craving fans.

Jack Coleman originally established his coffee brand in 2010, serving up from a stall in the food mecca Spa Terminus in Bermondsey. Coleman Coffee Roasters, his first permanent space, is housed in an old delicatessen and its previous life is evident in the layout of the small venue with large shop-front windows and a unique terrazzo marble floor.

Although what is on offer at this pretty café is limited, every item has been selected personally by Jack for its delicious taste and aesthetic appeal. The South American beans have been roasted in-house and have a velvety rich flavour, while accompanying snacks are irresistibly stacked on the bar including pastries from Little Bread Pedlar and particularly good Iranian nougat.

Coffee

We roast all of our
coffee on a 1950s
Otto Swadlo roaster
in Peckham

250g   £8
500g   £14
1 kilo   £28

Please ask the staff
advice about which
coffee suits your
home brewing method

We can also grind
it for you.

WHITE CUBE
—
Gallery

144-152 Bermondsey Street, Southwark, SE1 3TQ
020 7930 5373
whitecube.com

White Cube, with Jay Jopling at the helm, built its reputation with the 1990s Brit Art phenomenon. The gallery has two London spaces that display a broad roster of international, avant-garde artists. Both galleries are free to enter and the exhibitions change every month.

Their huge Bermondsey space opened in 2011 in a former warehouse. The monumental stark building stands out among the quaint terraced streets, with hangar-like spaces housing works of colossal scale and impact. Some of the most notable exhibitions include the atmospheric installations of Anselm Kiefer and mesmerising video masterworks of Christian Marclay.

White Cube Bermondsey is the perfect place to pop into for a moment of calm and artistic reflection, perhaps between shopping and eating in the area. Great nearby restaurants include José, Casse-Croûte and Flour & Grape, while Borough Market is another foodie neighbour.

MONMOUTH

—

Coffee Shop

2 Park Street, The Borough, Southwark, SE1 9AB
020 7232 3010
monmouthcoffee.co.uk

Monmouth was the pioneering force in speciality coffee in London. The artisan company started roasting and retailing in 1978 in the basement of their tiny Covent Garden store, before opening a second, more expansive space in Borough Market.

The team travels extensively to source the best beans from single estate farms. Through their growing business, Monmouth leads the way in promoting sustainable farming and egalitarian trading. This thoughtful process ensures they serve only the finest quality coffee, and has given the brand a cult status.

The Borough branch is grand and welcoming, with a pick'n'mix-style counter of fragrant beans to buy, and a barista station for freshly made coffee to drink. The café is always busy with locals and tourists alike, enjoying some of the best coffee and pastries in London.

Aside from serving and selling coffee and beans in London, the company also provides beans to quality conscious cafés and shops all over the UK.

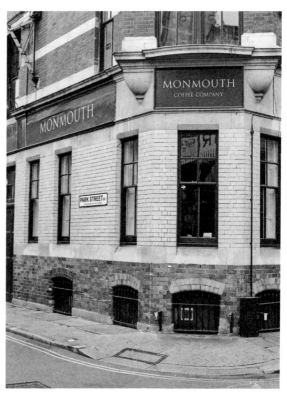

DUDDELL'S

—

Restaurant

9a St. Thomas Street, Southwark, SE1 9RY
020 3957 9932
duddells.co/london

Some of the most fun dining experiences in London can be found in Chinatown, where Londoners and tourists feast on dim sum and Chinese specialities. However, for an extra-special Chinese meal, head to London Bridge where Hong Kong export Duddell's has set up shop.

The original Duddell's restaurant is in Hong Kong and holds a Michelin star; its London counterpart is located in the historic Grade II listed St Thomas' Church, which has been beautifully restored by Michaelis Boyd. The space, spread over two floors, celebrates its heritage features while contemporary accents and pastel colours add a punch of retro-modernism.

The menu features authentic Cantonese dishes with a creative twist. The delicate dim sum are colourful and delicious, but the star of the show is the crispy duck, which is in limited supply each day.

Duddell's also has regularly changing art exhibitions, so be sure to have a look around when you visit.

LIBRERIA

—

Shop

65 Hanbury Street, Brick Lane, E1 5JP
libreria.io

Libreria on Hanbury Street in East London is a mecca for book lovers. The shop is by Second Home, the brainchild of Rohan Silva, who wanted to create an uncomplicated sanctuary for bibliophiles. You won't find a café or any wifi here.

The intriguing building has been transformed by Spanish architects SelgasCano and is an interpretation of Jorge Luis Borges' short story The Library of Babel. It is a compact space that has been cleverly designed to give the illusion of endless bookshelves. The mirrored walls and bright yellow interiors are a bold but brilliant décor choice, quite unlike any other conventional London bookshop.

The books are carefully categorised into unexpected themes, like 'wanderlust' and 'the city', in the hope of introducing customers to a new collection of titles they may not have otherwise encountered.

LYLE'S

—

Restaurant

Tea Building, 56 Shoreditch High Street, Shoreditch, E1 6JJ
020 3011 5911
lyleslondon.com

Lyle's has become a staple restaurant for discerning eaters in East London. The restaurant is housed in Shoreditch's Tea Building, a former tea factory. The industrial style open-plan dining room benefits from masses of natural daylight thanks to the large Crittall windows.

The white walls, poured concrete floors and simple classic wooden tables allow nothing to distract from the main event; the beautifully inventive micro-seasonal food. Chef James Lowe opened the space in 2014 after four years at St. John Bread & Wine. At lunchtime a variety of imaginative small plates are on offer, while at dinner a set four course menu changes daily. The kitchen prides itself on using only the best produce; fish is delivered daily from Cornwall and in the summer the chefs travel to the south coast to pick fruit.

James also runs The Guest Series at Lyle's, inviting chefs from exciting eateries around the world to cook for a night or two. With this programme, he hopes to inspire foreign chefs and educate his diners with the very best of British cuisine and ingredients.

BLUE MOUNTAIN SCHOOL

—

Interdisciplinary Space

9 Chance Street, Shoreditch, E2 7JB
020 7739 9733
bluemountain.school

Redchurch Street is one of Shoreditch's most popular streets with an ever-growing family of boutiques, hipster hotels and cafés. It is the ideal home for Blue Mountain School, an ultra cool, high-end interdisciplinary space that opened in April 2018, a new venture that evolved from the boundary-pushing retail store Hostem, originally founded in 2010.

The space feels exclusive and luxurious, and is dedicated to a carefully curated selection of fashion, design, art, food and music. Explore the wonder-filled six floors and discover immaculate garments by Anecho, Amy Revier and Geoffrey B. Small, a seasonal dinner menu at Mãos by Nuno Mendes and a perfume atelier by Lyn Harris of Perfumer H.

Memorable pieces include furniture by Valentin Loellmann, who has entirely designed and realised the upper floors of the building, ceramics by BDDW from Tyler Hay's Philadelphia studio, and artworks in Blue Projects - the dedicated exhibition arm of Blue Mountain School - which has featured shows by Elias Hansen and Alex Olson.

The Blue Mountain School team also owns the New Road Residence in Whitechapel, a beautifully refurbished Georgian East London home with three bedrooms, available to rent for the ultimate stylish city stay.

OZONE COFFEE ROASTERS

—

Coffee Shop

11 Leonard Street, Shoreditch, EC2A 4AQ
020 7490 1039
ozonecoffee.co.uk

Old Street station is a hub of activity with lots of exciting young pop-ups. The area changed hugely when many businesses moved their offices to 'Silicon Roundabout' and restaurants followed in quick succession.

Ozone Coffee Roasters was founded in New Zealand in 1998 and opened in London in 2012. The industrial-style roastery and café soon became a favourite with locals working in the area. Ozone's speciality coffee is roasted onsite and is served in cafés all over Europe. The baristas are some of the best in the city at brewing and pouring, and both the espresso based drinks and pour-over options are worth trying. There are also house-made sodas and Good & Proper Tea for non-coffee drinkers.

Alongside the unbeatable coffee, Ozone serves a tasty brunch menu throughout the day. Choose from a selection of irresistible dishes; we recommend the Seeded Granola with burnt honey yoghurt and Yorkshire rhubarb or the Omelette with roast kumara, chard & mushroom, sumac yoghurt and fried shallots.

COFFEE →

MON-FRI   7.00-10.00
SAT-SUN   8.30-5.30

NO SMOKING

THE MARKSMAN PUBLIC HOUSE
—
Restaurant & Pub

254 Hackney Road, Hackney, E2 7SJ
020 7739 7393
marksmanpublichouse.com

After spending a sunny Sunday morning wandering through the colourful Columbia Road Flower Market, there is no better place to stop for lunch than The Marksman. This traditional, no-fuss British pub occupies a corner spot on Hackney Road, a street awash with celebrated eateries.

The Marksman is a favourite with locals - who enjoy reduced-price pints - and a must for foodies visiting this area of East London. On the ground floor the glossy, wood-panelling and green leather banquettes are inviting and comforting, while upstairs there is a refined and modern dining room for dinner. For a more intimate experience, the 'Cellar Room' is a private dining area and chef's table that seats up to 12 guests.

The food, from chef-owners Tom Harris and Jon Rotheram, is reliably excellent. Settle down for a hearty lunch, such as Pigeon & Gravy, and don't miss the addictive Brown Butter & Honey Tart. There is always an interesting selection of local brews to keep your thirst quenched.

BACON BUNS

BAKED GOODS

TEA & COFFEE

EAT-IN

TAKE-AWAY

Marksman

CONSERVATORY ARCHIVES

—

Shop

493-495 Hackney Road, Bethnal Green, E2 9ED
07785 522 762
conservatoryarchives.co.uk

This curious plant shop is an emporium of all things green. Part of the community of Hackney Road creatives, Conservatory Archives was set-up by Jin Ahn and Giacomo Plazzotta in 2015 as a place for plant-lovers to browse and buy beautiful botanicals.

The shop is an oasis of calm and creativity. Mid-century furniture is interspersed with giant monsteras and cacti. Whether you want a decorative hanging plant or a tiny pot plant for your mantelpiece, there is greenery for every occasion available here. The staff are always able to offer handy advice on how to look after your plants and keep them happy and healthy. Conservatory Archives often collaborate with like-minded brands, creating and constructing immersive installations for shops, restaurants and art shows.

The team travel frequently, sourcing interesting and unusual plants from all over Europe, so there is always something new to be inspired by. Let Conservatory Archives transport you to another world, leafy and lovely.

POPHAMS BAKERY

—

Bakery

19 Prebend Street, Islington, N1 8PF
pophamsbakery.com

London has upped its pastry game in recent years, a trend that is led by North London bakery Pophams. Located down an unlikely street in Islington, many make the pilgrimage to Pophams every weekend to pick up the finest flaky croissants in town.

The bakery was founded by Ollie Gold in 2017; with the help of head chef Florin Grama, he aims to share his love of the finest sourdough breads and interesting pastries. Many of the flavours and inspirations come from Ollie's travels and previous experience working in the hospitality industry. The team starts baking at 2am and the specials often sell out within a few hours of opening.

Initially it was the indulgent maple bacon swirl that was most in demand, but as the Pophams team introduces more seasonal revelations to the menu, the list of must-have pastries is expanding. Alongside the inimitable artisan treats, Pophams serves Ozone coffee and a variety of high quality teas and hot chocolate.

PAPER MACHE TIGER

—

Shop

26 Cross Street, Islington, N1 2BG
020 7729 9620
papermachetiger.com

Islington is a lovely area to shop and browse. Upper Street, the main thoroughfare, runs through the centre of the neighbourhood, and is a parade of laid-back eateries and boutique brands.

Slightly off the beaten track, Paper Mache Tiger combines concept shop and café in a transformed former pencil factory. The company, originally founded in 2008 as a fashion sales and communications agency, opened their first store to showcase their own designs alongside exciting emerging designers from around the world. The shop has a conscious curation of both womens' and menswear, with sustainable fashion from New Yorker Mara Hoffman and luxury cashmere from Allude.

The bright white space is decorated with whimsical plants and foliage giving a relaxed vibe that encourages visitors to wander and explore. When you have finished shopping, sit back and admire your purchases in the café and enjoy coffee from South London roastery, Assembly.

CORNERSTONE

—

Restaurant

3 Prince Edward Road, Hackney, E9 5LX
020 8986 3922
cornerstonehackney.com

After six years working for master fish chef Nathan Outlaw in his Michelin-starred restaurants in Cornwall and London, Tom Brown opened his own restaurant, Cornerstone, in 2018. Unsurprisingly, his first solo venture aims to offer fresh, creative seafood in a relaxed setting.

Brown hails from Cornwall, where arguably the best fish is on offer, and he uses his experience of this bounty to bring flavours of the sea to Hackney Wick. The venue is contemporary and industrial in style, with a central kitchen giving a touch of drama to the room.

Some of Cornerstone's recipes - like the Potted Shrimp Crumpet and the Pickled Oysters with celery and horseradish - have been on the menu since opening, but most of the dishes change in response to the availability of produce. Brown is sensitive but daring in his treatment of subtle fish flavours, often combining unlikely ingredient combinations to create dishes that are inimitably brilliant and delicious.

MOMOSAN SHOP

—

Shop

79a Wilton Way, Hackney, E8 1BG
020 7249 4989
momosanshop.com

Momosan Shop, in Hackney, is a sanctuary of beauty and design. The small store is found on Wilton Way, a hidden hub of independent shops and boutique cafés. Neighbours include creative dining concept Pidgin and cake sensation Violet Bakery.

Owner Momoko Mizutani was born in Japan and moved to London to study design at Central Saint Martins. After working with classic designers like Ally Capellino, Momoko decided to open her own store, Momosan Shop, in 2011. The boutique found its current home in Shoreditch in 2014.

Thoughtful, functional items are painstakingly organised on the shop shelves. Momoko picks her items with heritage and quality in mind, selecting the work of craftsmen that she knows and loves. Her store exhibits a range of items, small and large, with something to suit every budget. The selection includes delicate glassware by Jochen Holz, pottery by Shun Kadohashi and socks by A Woven Plane.

Whether you intend to shop or not, you will leave this tiny store feeling refreshed and inspired.

P. FRANCO

—

Wine Bar & Restaurant

107 Lower Clapton Road, Hackney, E5 0NP
020 8533 4660
pfranco.co.uk

Whenever you are in East London, it is worth the detour to Clapton for P. Franco. This welcoming venue has become known for its creative wine cellar, relaxed atmosphere and exciting chef collaborations.

Innovative owners Liam Kelleher and James Noble opened P. Franco in a former Chinese takeaway shop in 2014. A year later, the small team began pushing the boundaries of what a tiny wine bar could offer by inviting talented chefs from internationally-renowned restaurants to cook up their favourite creations on the restrictive two induction hobs. Some of the most popular guest chefs to date include Tim Spedding, formerly sous-chef at Michelin-starred Clove Club, and Anna Tobias who previously worked at Rochelle Canteen and The River Café.

The Latin name, P. Franco, refers to the process where vines are grown on their own root stocks, ensuring a certain quality and flavour to the wine. The small bar has shelves of intriguing bottles and the knowledgeable staff will help you choose a glass of something delicious.

The team's second venture, Bright, is a fully-fledged restaurant in London Fields. Here they serve a more comprehensive menu complemented by an excellent wine list.

HECKFIELD PLACE

—

Hotel - Countryside Escape

Hampshire, RG27 0LD
0118 932 6868
heckfieldplace.com

London has everything and more to entertain you for a lifetime, but city dwellers often take advantage of the nearby counties for their calming countryside and fresh air.

Heckfield Place is a bucolic luxury weekend escape, just an hour's drive from West London, or an easy train journey from the city. The Georgian house has benefitted from a decade of thoughtful restoration and is surrounded by 400 acres of tranquil rural landscape.

There are 45 bedrooms and suites, which have all enjoyed the magic touch of designer Ben Thompson. The rooms are rustic but stylish, with immaculate details wherever you look. Perhaps the most spectacular is the 'Long Room', an extravagant suite that features a portrait of Virginia Woolf.

The restaurant is headed up by Skye Gyngell, who made a name for herself and won a Michelin star at Petersham Nurseries. Her food utilises the bountiful produce of the hotel's gardens, with an emphasis on hearty seasonal dishes. A small spa hideaway features products by Wildsmith and there is a gym managed by Bodyism for fitness and wellbeing.

Guests can enjoy wild lake swimming, bicycle rides, screenings in the boutique cinema, or take part in workshops, events and talks in 'The Assembly'.

CLARE SMYTH

—

CHEF, CORE

Born in Northern Ireland, Clare grew up on a farm in County Antrim where her lifelong love and passion for food began. At 15, she began working in one of the best restaurants in Northern Ireland, and at 16 she moved to England to further develop her skills to become a world-class chef. In 2002, Clare joined Restaurant Gordon Ramsay, and in 2005 she left London to gain experience abroad at Alain Ducasse's renowned Le Louis XV in Monaco. In 2007, aged just 28, she returned to London as Head Chef at Restaurant Gordon Ramsay and became the first female chef in the UK to run a restaurant with three Michelin stars. In 2012, she was promoted to Chef Patron. In 2013, Clare was appointed Member of the Order of the British Empire (MBE) for services to the hospitality industry, and she and her team went on to win numerous awards and recognitions.

Clare opened her first solo restaurant, Core, in August 2017 in the heart of Notting Hill. In its first year, Core was named 'Best Restaurant' at the GQ Food and Drink Awards and was the highest ever new entry - receiving a perfect 10 - in the Good Food Guide 2019 edition.

In 2018, Clare was awarded two Michelin stars for Core as a new entry in the 2019 Michelin Guide, was named World's Best Female Chef by the World's 50 Best Restaurants, and she cooked for Meghan and Harry at the Royal Wedding.

What is your earliest memory of food and was food an important part of your childhood?
Food was a very important part of my childhood. I grew up close to nature on a farm in Northern Ireland and was always surrounded with fresh ingredients and produce. Many of my childhood memories revolve around the smell of fresh baked soda and wheaten breads.

Was a career in the kitchen an obvious and easy choice for you?
Yes, absolutely. By the age of 15, I knew I wanted to be a chef at the top level. My parents were farmers and I don't think they really understood what I wanted to do. Coming from a family where food was important, but very simple and humble, haute cuisine and gastronomy were not in our family at all.

I finished school and the next day moved to England and I got myself into college and in an

apprenticeship straight away. My parents really worried about me and wanted me to come home but I knew I wanted to be a chef.

How has the restaurant industry in London changed since you started out?
In the last 10-15 years it has exploded and become much more diverse. The restaurant scene is changing so fast and there are great restaurants all over London. There are also so many better food producers in the UK growing specific little things and there is a big difference in the kinds of ingredients you can get. Gastronomy in the UK is exciting.

Why did you choose to open your first solo venture in London, rather than anywhere else in the world?
London is home for me. I've always loved this city. It is a great city to have a business because there is a huge population of people who live here

and so many people travel here for business and pleasure. Since opening Core, we've been full all the time.

How do you define your cuisine at Core?

Modern British fine dining. Our menu at Core has an emphasis on natural, sustainable food sourced from the UK's most dedicated farmers and food producers.

How have your experiences of cooking in restaurants around the world influenced your style?

My training was predominately in classical French cookery so my root is that, but I am certainly influenced by simplicity and purity of different styles of food and how that can be translated into British cuisine.

What is your favourite dish on the menu at Core?

The 'Potato and roe' dish is our signature dish. Not only do the potatoes come from a grower that I have been working with for about 15 years, but it's inspired by my childhood. My family has one of the biggest potato farms in Northern Ireland so I grew up eating potatoes every single day. The farm was also by the coast - hence the roe. Even now I eat a potato every day before service at Core. It is an expression of where I am from and who I am today.

What are your favourite ingredients to cook with and why?

I am passionate about vegetable cookery, but I don't really have favourite ingredients, it's really about the seasons for me. I take inspiration from nature and use ingredients from the height of the season and we really try to celebrate what we have available on our doorstep.

What do you want people to feel while experiencing one of your meals?

Enjoyment. I want them to have a great time and feel relaxed. It is about feeling at home - dining with best friends in your home with amazing food and wine.

Which chefs do you admire and why?

Throughout my career I have always looked up to Gordon Ramsay. I've worked with him for so many years and he has always been incredibly supportive of me. I love Thomas Keller's style, he is a real gentleman and a perfectionist. I also look up to Alain Ducasse, he is one of the greatest chefs in history. His cooking style is phenomenal - he has no fear and his style always evolves and changes. He will leave behind a huge legacy for chefs in years to come.

What do you think makes London's food scene one of the best in the world?

It is the quality and diversity of the restaurants that are available in all areas of London. The restaurants push each other to become better - it is a very exciting dining scene.

Where do you go to eat when you have some time off?

I like Bentley's Oyster Bar & Grill for oysters and Champagne. I also like Scott's in Mayfair, and if I want to go out closer to home, I'll go to Trinity in Clapham. I also love lots of Asian food so I'll go somewhere like A. Wong.

If you could eat in one restaurant in the world what would it be?

I would love to go to El Bulli but unfortunately it doesn't exist anymore! I would also like to go to Frantzen in Stockholm.

What advice would you give to chefs starting up in London?

Put your head down, focus and work hard. And, work in the best places you can so you can learn from the most successful in the business.

Lastly, if you were on a desert island and only allowed three ingredients, what would you take?

Parmesan, Perigord truffles and Barolo vinegar.

XAVIER BRAY

—

DIRECTOR, THE WALLACE COLLECTION

Xavier Bray had an artistic upbringing, living and studying in a number of European countries as a child. He studied Art History and Anthropology at University College London. Inspired by London's rich and diverse art scene, Xavier quickly realised he wanted to work within the world of museums.

After a brief stint at Sotheby's, he developed a particular interest in Spanish art and completed a PhD on Francisco Goya, the 18th century Spanish artist. Xavier then spent a year working in Madrid, at the Prado, and then at the National Gallery in London. It was at Dulwich Picture Gallery that Xavier had the freedom to experiment and curate smaller, more specialist exhibitions. In 2016, Xavier joined the Wallace Collection as Director. While maintaining and treasuring the Wallace artworks, Xavier is also helping to promote this important and precious collection to new and wider audiences.

Can you tell us a bit about your background – did art play an important part in your early life?
It was crucial. My father was a journalist so he was posted in different countries every three or four years. We lived in Brussels, Paris, Madrid and Rome. My mother animated art for children so she used us as guinea pigs, to look at things in each of those countries. My first real awakening to the beauty of art and architecture was in Rome when my mother, quite madly, would cycle us around the streets to see the wonderful churches and architecture.

Growing up I went to many different schools and nothing really struck me, but when I discovered A-Level Art History existed I was completely amazed – it all clicked and made sense.

What brought you to the Wallace Collection?
I knew the Wallace Collection as a student and I remember being brought here, but I'm afraid I was probably one of those people who took the museum for granted. When I was preparing for the interview I saw the collection with fresh eyes. It got me really excited about applying for the job. The Wallace Collection was yet to be exploited, to put it crudely. It was like finding a

goldmine that was yet to be discovered by so many people so it was really exciting. I went for the job and amazingly got it.

What is your vision for the museum?
The first thing is to make people realise how lucky we, the British public, are to have been given this collection in 1897 by Sir Richard Wallace and his wife. They inherited the collection, looked after and added to it, and then they gave it to the nation. That was the first thing I really wanted people to know; this is yours, it belongs to everyone, which is quite unique in London. You can walk into the museum for free and just enjoy the extraordinary artworks.

What do you want people to feel or learn while experiencing the museum?
I want people to feel a mixture of being overwhelmed and having a sense of discovery – to find an intimacy within certain spaces or rooms, and to maybe engage with one object and find out all about it. I want people to discover things, and feel that it's okay to only have, say, half an hour to see a bit but then to come back to see more.

Why do you think it is important for people to discover art in general?

It's like reading a good book or poem, or listening to a good piece of music. Many people have forgotten how to look and spend time inside a painting or sculpture and let that piece of art speak back to them. People think you need knowledge to be able to do that, but I feel quite the contrary, that it is really important to understand and use the visual experience.

The building has been transformed with a recent exhibition space in the basement – can you tell us a bit about this?

The new exhibition space is like a theatre stage for the Wallace. We can take things from upstairs and show them in different ways. It gives us a flexibility that we haven't had before and means that we can be a bit more ambitious with our exhibition programme, which is a good way of attracting more attention and diversifying our audience.

In terms of the architecture, do you have a favourite room or space?

There are so many different kinds of spaces at the Wallace. The room that most intrigues me is also the space that I can't wait to transform – Sir Richard Wallace's smoking room, where he could retire with his friends and look at great pieces of art while smoking a cigar or hookah pipe.

The room still exists but the original Turkish tiles have almost all been stripped, there's only one small corner that remains intact. The big ambition would be to restore that room back to its original style and give it back its 'smoking room' feel.

If you had to name a favourite piece in the museum's collection, what would it be and why?

The piece that convinced me to apply for the job is the beautiful, gold Asante head; it's a very intriguing and important piece. It really made me think differently about what the Wallace represents; if you think the Wallace is just about 18th century paintings then think again.

What's your favourite London museum and why?

I think the V&A has always been my favourite. I like the way you can enter from different directions with no queuing. I find it increasingly annoying when there are restrictions on the route you have to take around a museum, I love museums that are just open and are easy for people to wander in and wander around.

Which museum in the world has had the biggest effect on you?

For me, the Prado is possibly the greatest gallery in the world. I always find it totally inspiring to look at the collection whenever I go to Madrid and it always fills me with delight. The Met is another of the greatest museums – I just love the encyclopaedic quality that it offers.

Finally, if you were allowed to add one piece to the museum's collection, what would it be?

Amazingly, in 1914 the Wallace was offered "The Burghers of Calais" by Rodin because he wanted to give something to the British government and we were approached because of the French connection that we had. The Wallace Collection said no - because they couldn't acquire any additional artworks - but I would probably have taken it on long-term loan and displayed it in the garden. It is one of the greatest sculptural groups ever made and would have really changed how people see the Wallace.

Some people think we are a private house, so don't come in. I'm keen to make more people realise that behind the beautiful townhouse entrance, there's a collection that belongs to everyone and that everyone can access.

FURTHER IDEAS

—

ESTATE OFFICE COFFEE
Charming café serving Allpress coffee alongside locally-made
pastries, bread and sweet treats.
1 Drewstead Road, Streatham, SW16 1LY
020 3627 0647
estateofficecoffee.co.uk

DULWICH PICTURE GALLERY
The world's first purpose-built gallery, in 1811, now hosts exciting
exhibitions and a permanent collection of Baroque masterpieces.
Gallery Road, Dulwich, SE21 7AD
020 8693 5254
dulwichpicturegallery.org.uk

OLD SPIKE ROASTERY
Social enterprise that offers training and jobs to the homeless,
while roasting and serving premium artisan coffee.
54 Peckham Rye, Peckham, SE15 4JR
hello@oldspikeroastery.com
oldspikeroastery.com

ALPHA SHADOWS
Selling an exclusive selection of men's clothing, contemporary ceramics
and handcrafted goods in the creative, mixed-use Bussey Building.
C1, The Bussey Building, 133 Copeland Road, Peckham, SE15 3SN
020 7635 3718
alphashadows.com

THE LASLETT
Boutique hotel with 51 rooms and suites spread across five
Grade II listed Victorian townhouses.
8 Pembridge Gardens, Notting Hill, W2 4DU
020 7792 6688
living-rooms.co.uk/hotel/the-laslett

WORKSHOP COFFEE
Just off Oxford Street, this charming café serves great coffee and homely food in a simple, flakeboard-furnished space.
1 Barrett Street, Marylebone, W1U 1AX
marylebone@workshopcoffee.com
workshopcoffee.com

CLIPSTONE
Relaxed, neighbourhood restaurant serving seasonal British dishes alongside a succinct, carefully-chosen drinks list including wines on tap.
5 Clipstone Street, Fitzrovia, W1W 6BB
020 7637 0871
clipstonerestaurant.co.uk

FOLK
Contemporary casualware for men and women in neighbouring shops on a pedestrianised, independent-focussed shopping street.
49 & 53 Lamb's Conduit Street, Holborn, WC1N 3NG
020 7404 6458
folkclothing.com

PADELLA
No reservations cult pasta bar near Borough Market, serving delicious, reasonably-priced antipasti and pasta dishes.
6 Southwark Street, Southwark, SE1 1TQ
info@padella.co
padella.co

JOSÉ
Cosy tapas and sherry bar on Bermondsey Street, by critically-acclaimed Spanish chef José Pizarro.
104 Bermondsey Street, Southwark, SE1 3UB
020 7403 4902
josepizarro.com/jose-tapas-bar

40 MALTBY STREET

Rustic dishes and natural wine in a relaxed venue under
the railway arches, just south of London Bridge.
40 Maltby Street, Southwark, SE1 3PA
020 7237 9247
40maltbystreet.com

THE GIBSON

Flamboyant cocktails by mixologists formerly of The Connaught and
Nightjar, in an intimate, prohibition-themed venue.
44 Old Street, Clerkenwell, EC1V 9AQ
020 7608 2774
thegibsonbar.london

THE HOXTON

The original hotel from the creative group, with rooms ranging from
'shoebox' to 'roomy' plus two restaurants and communal spaces.
81 Great Eastern Street, Shoreditch, EC2A 3HU
020 7550 1000
thehoxton.com

BRAT

Michelin-starred restaurant headed up by Tomos Parry, serving
Basque-inspired dishes cooked on an open wood fire grill.
First floor, 4 Redchurch Street, Shoreditch, E1 6JL
hello@bratrestaurant.com
bratrestaurant.com

LABOUR AND WAIT

An independent brand housed in a striking green-tiled building, with
a selection of new and vintage household goods and stationery.
85 Redchurch Street, Shoreditch, E2 7DJ
020 7729 6253
labourandwait.co.uk

ROCHELLE CANTEEN

Café and restaurant offering a concise, modern menu in a former
school that now hosts a collection of creative businesses.
16 Playground Gardens, Shoreditch, E2 7FA
020 7729 5677
arnoldandhenderson.com/rochelle-canteen

BRAWN

Daylight-filled, minimal dining room on Columbia Road, serving a
daily-changing menu of seasonal, produce-driven dishes.
49 Columbia Road, Bethnal Green, E2 7RG
020 7729 5692
brawn.co

CLIMPSON & SONS

Cult café that sources, roasts and crafts some of the
finest coffees in East London.
67 Broadway Market, Hackney, E8 4PH
020 7254 7199
climpsonandsons.com

UNTITLED

Innovative cocktails by master mixologist Tony Conigliaro, alongside
Japanese-inspired food, in a raw, minimalist space.
538 Kingsland Road, Hackney, E8 4AH
07841 022 924
untitled-bar.com

JOLENE

Restaurant with onsite bakery, from the team behind renowned
neighbourhood restaurants Primeur and Westerns Laundry.
21 Newington Green, Hackney, N16 9PU
020 3887 2309
jolenen16.com

WEEKEND JOURNALS

Editor: Milly Kenny-Ryder
thoroughlymodernmilly.com

Designer: Simon Lovell

Photographer: Gabriel Kenny-Ryder
gabrielkennyryder.com

All venues have been visited personally.

Thank you to Chris and Mark for your support and input.

Published in the United Kingdom in November 2018.

ISBN: 978-1-9998591-3-8 (paperback)
ISBN: 978-1-9998591-4-5 (hardback)

© Weekend Journals Ltd

All photographs by Gabriel Kenny-Ryder.

Copyright Information:
p.15-17 photos taken with permission from Royal Botanic Gardens, Kew; p.31 (bottom-right) KEEP OUT OF REACH OF CHILDREN (2018) by Danielle Dean, Installation view of KNOCK KNOCK at South London Gallery; p.31 (top-left) Others, 2011 © Maurizio Cattelan; p.59-61 all artworks © The Wallace Collection; p.81 all photos taken with permission from White Cube, (bottom-right) © Doris Salcedo; p.92 (left) Jennefer Hoffmann, October 12, 2017, unglazed light and dark stoneware, 32 cm x 28 cm; (right) Luke Eastop, Quadric Vase Range, British buff stoneware and porcelain, sizes variable; (right) Nancy Kwon, Tea Bowl 3, ochre stoneware and clear gloss, 8.5 cm x 10 cm.

Printed by Taylor Bros Bristol on FSC approved uncoated paper

hello@weekendjournals.co.uk
weekendjournals.co.uk